My Bilingual Talking Dictionary

Romanian & English

First published in 2005 by Mantra Lingua
Global House, 303 Ballards Lane, London N12 8NP
www.mantralingua.com

This TalkingPEN edition 2009
Text copyright © 2005 Mantra Lingua
Illustrations copyright © 2005 Mantra Lingua
(except pages 4-9, 42-49 Illustrations copyright © 2005 Priscilla Lamont)
Audio copyright © 2009 Mantra Lingua

With thanks to the illustrators:
David Anstey, Dixie Bedford-Stockwell, Louise Daykin,
Alison Hopkins, Richard Johnson, Allan Jones,
Priscilla Lamont, Yokococo

A CIP record for this book is available from the British Library

Hear each page of this talking book narrated with the RecorderPEN!
1) To get started touch the arrow button below with the RecorderPEN.
2) To hear the word in English touch the 'E' button at the top of the pages.
3) To hear the word spoken in an English sentence touch the 'S' button at the top of the pages.
4) To hear the language of your choice touch the 'L' button on the top of the pages.
5) Touch the square button below to hear more information about using the Dictionary with the RecorderPEN.

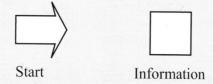

Start   Information

Contents

Cuprins

Myself

ochi
oki
eyes

păr
puhr
hair

gură
gooruh
mouth

urechi
oo-reki
ears

dinți
dints
teeth

mână
munuh
hand

degetul mare
deh-jet-ool mareh
thumb

încheietura mâinii
unqueyeh-toorah mewnee
wrist

degete
deh-jet-eh
fingers

talie
tahllyeh
waist

picioare
pitch-woreh
feet

degetele de la picioare
deh-jet-eleh deh lah pitch-woreh
toes

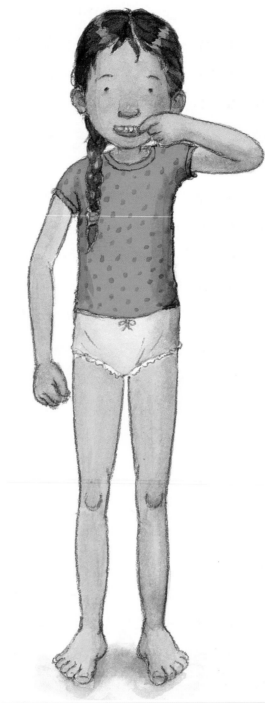

fericit
ferry-chit
happy

trist
trist
sad

supărat
soupuh-rat
angry

gelos
geloss
jealous

bucuros
boo-koo-ross
excited

4

Eu însumi

cap
cap
head

față
fatsuh
face

ceafă
chya-fuh
neck

nas
nars
nose

umeri
oo-mery
shoulders

braț
brats
arm

cot
cot
elbow

stomac
sto-mack
stomach

spate
spateh
back

genunchi
gen-oonki
knee

picior
pitch-or
leg

gleznă
glehznuh
ankle

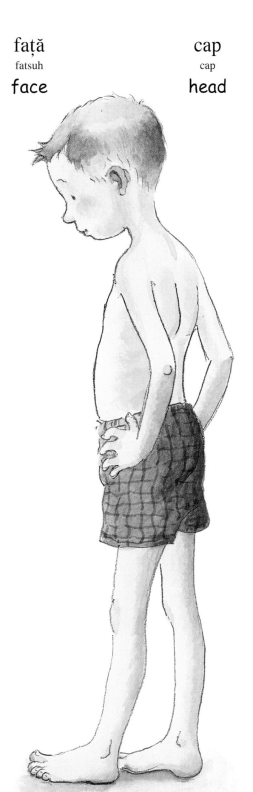

bolnav
bowl-nav
sick

foame
fwameh
hungry

speriat
spehryat
scared

timid
tee-mid
shy

obosit
oh-boss-it
tired

5

Clothes

palton
pal-ton
coat

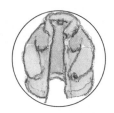

fular
foolahr
scarf

tricou
tri-cow
t-shirt

rochie
roky-eh
dress

fustă
foostuh
skirt

cardigan
cardigahn
cardigan

costum de baie
costoom deh bi-yeh
swimming costume

dres
dress
tights

chiloți
kilots
knickers

pantofi
pantof
shoes

Îmbrăcăminte

mănuși
munoosh
gloves

șapcă
shahp-kuh
hat

cămașă
kuh-mushuh
shirt

pulover
pull-over
jumper

pantaloni
pantahlon
trousers

pantaloni scurți
pantahlon skoorts
shorts

chiloți de baie
kilots deh bi-yeh
swimming trunks

șosete
shoseh-teh
socks

chiloți
kilots
underpants

tenisi
tenish
trainers

Family

Familia

bunică
boony-kuh
grandmother

bunic
boonyk
grandfather

bunic
boonyk
grandfather

bunică
boony-kuh
grandmother

mătușă
muht-ooshuh
aunt

tată
tatuh
father

mamă
mamuh
mother

unchi
oonki
uncle

frate
frah-teh
brother

soră
soruh
sister

fiu
fee-oo
son

fică
fee/kuh
daughter

copilaș
copy-lash
baby

Home

Locuința

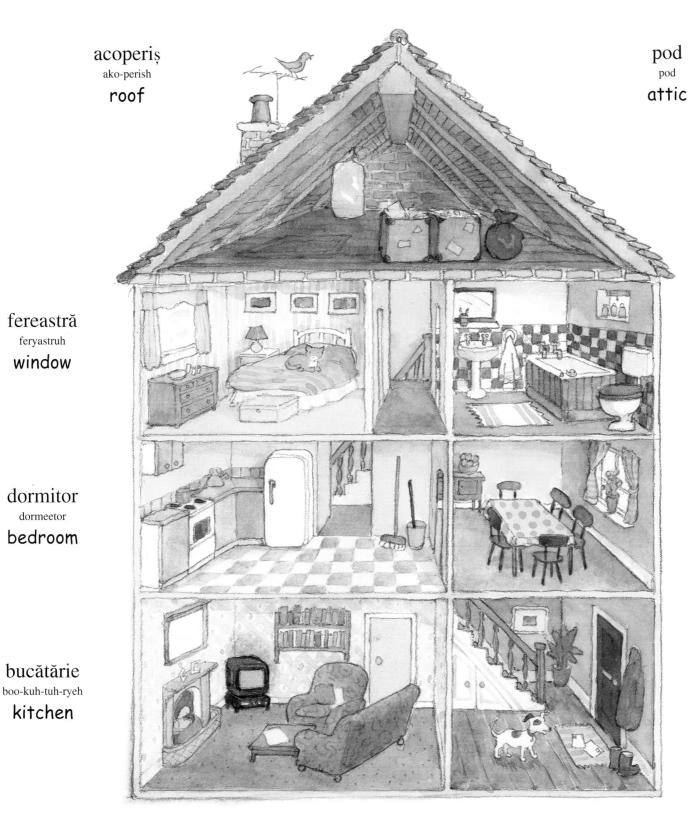

acoperiș
ako-perish
roof

pod
pod
attic

fereastră
feryastruh
window

camera de baie
camera deh bi-yeh
bathroom

dormitor
dormeetor
bedroom

sufragerie
soofrager-yeh
dining room

bucătărie
boo-kuh-tuh-ryeh
kitchen

hol
hole
hallway

perete
perehteh
wall

camera de zi
camera deh zee
lounge/living room

scară
skaruh
staircase

ușă
ooshuh
door

House and Contents

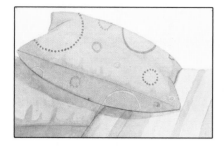

perna
pernuh
pillow

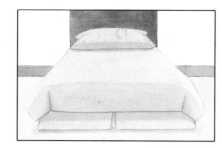

pat
pat
bed

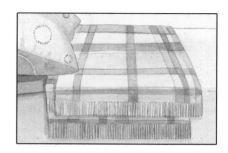

patura
puh-tooruh
blanket

coș de gunoi
kosh deh goonoy
bin

ventilator
ventilahtor
fan

lampa
lampuh
lamp

telefon
telefon
telephone

mașina de spalat rufe
mashinuh deh spuhlaht roofeh
washing machine

prajitor de paine
pruh-zhi-tor deh puh-ineh
toaster

ceainic
tcha-ee-nick
kettle

robinet
robineht
tap

frigider
fridgee-der
fridge

aragaz
ah-rah-gas
cooker

chiuveta
queue-veh-tuh
sink

calorifer
calorie-fer
radiator

baie
bi-yeh
bath

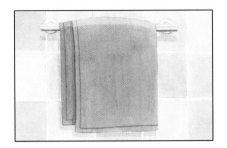

prosop
pro-soap
towel

oglindă
oglinduh
mirror

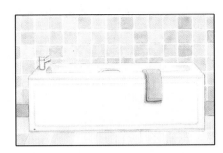

toaletă
twa-letuh
toilet

hîrtie igienică
hur-tyeh eej-yeneekuh
toilet roll

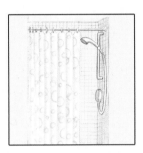

duș
doosh
shower

televizor
tele-vee-zor
television

radio
rah-dio
radio

draperii
drah-per-ee
curtains

dulap
dool-up
cupboard

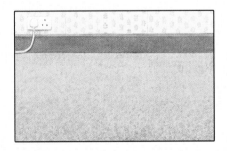

mochetă
moch-ketuh
carpet

sofa
so-fa
sofa

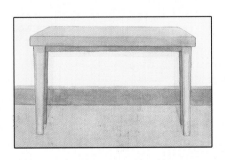

masă
massuh
table

Fruit

banană
bananuh
banana

papaia
papaya
papaya

pară
paruh
pear

pepene
peh-peh-neh
melon

prună
proonuh
plum

lămâie
luh-muh-yeh
lemon

cireșe
chiresheh
cherries

căpșuni
kuhpshoon
strawberries

Fructe

struguri
stroo-goor
grapes

ananas
ah-nah-nass
pineapple

mangotier
mangotier
mango

portocală
portokaluh
orange

piersică
pee-yer-sikuh
peach

măr
muhr
apple

laicis
lychees
lychees

rodie
rodyeh
pomegranate

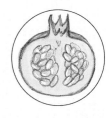

Vegetables

ceapă
chyapuh
onion

conopidă
konopeeduh
cauliflower

cartof
kar-toff
potato

porumb
poroomb
sweetcorn

ciupercă
chew-per-kuh
mushroom

roșie
roshyeh
tomato

fasole
fassoleh
beans

ridiche
ree-dee-keh
radish

Legume

usturoi
oos-too-roy
garlic

dovleac
dov-lyak
pumpkin/squash

castravete
kas-tra-veh-teh
cucumber

conopidă italiană
konopeeduh italianuh
broccoli

ardei
arday
pepper/capsicum

morcov
morkov
carrot

salată
salatuh
lettuce

mazăre
mazuh-reh
peas

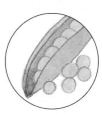

15

Food and Drink

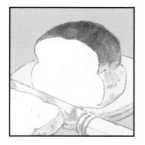

pâine
puh-ineh
bread

unt
oont
butter

gem
gem
jam

sandviș
sand-vish
sandwich

zahăr
za-huhr
sugar

miere
myeh-reh
honey

fulgi
foolgi
cereal

lapte
lap-teh
milk

tăieței
tuh-yeh-tsay
noodles

orez
orehz
rice

spaghete
spaghetteh
spaghetti

pița
pitsa
pizza

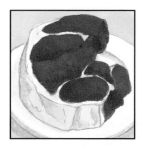

carne
carneh
meat

pește
peh-shteh
fish

ou
oh
egg

brânză
br-unzuh
cheese

ciocolată
chyo-colahtuh
chocolate

bomboane
bom-bwa-neh
sweets

prăjitură
pruh-zhi-tooruh
cake

budincă
boodinkuh
pudding

iaurt
yowrt
yoghurt

înghețată
un-gets-atuh
ice cream

biscuite
bis-koo-y-teh
biscuit

cartofi prăjiți
car-toff pruh-zhits
crisps

cartofi prăjiți
car-toff pruh-zhits
chips

sos picant
sauce pick-ant
ketchup

muștar
moosh-tar
mustard

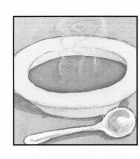

supă
soupuh
soup

suc de fructe
sook deh frookteh
fruit juice

apă minerală
apuh minerahluh
mineral water

sare
sahreh
salt

piper
pee-per
pepper

Meal Time

cuțit
koo-tseet
knife

furculiță
foor-cool-eetsuh
fork

lingură
leen-gooruh
spoon

bețișoare chinezești
betsy-shwo-are kineh-zehsht
chopsticks

cană
kanuh
mug

ceașcă
chya-shkuh
cup

pahar
pah-har
glass

La masă

farfurie
far-fooryeh
plate

farfurie adâncă
far-fooryeh adunkuh
bowl

cratiță
krateetsuh
saucepan

tigaie chinezească
tee-gahyeh kinehzyaskuh
wok

tigaie
tee-gahyeh
frying pan

termos
termos
flask

**cutie pentru
transportat prânzul**
kootyeh pent-roo
transportaht prunzool
lunchbox

Town

supermarket
sooper-market
supermarket

parcare
parc-areh
car park

centru sportiv
chent-roo sportiv
sports centre

bibliotecă
bee-blee-o-techkuh
library

post de poliție
post deh poli-tsyeh
police station

gară
garruh
train station

post de pompieri
post deh pomp-yer
fire station

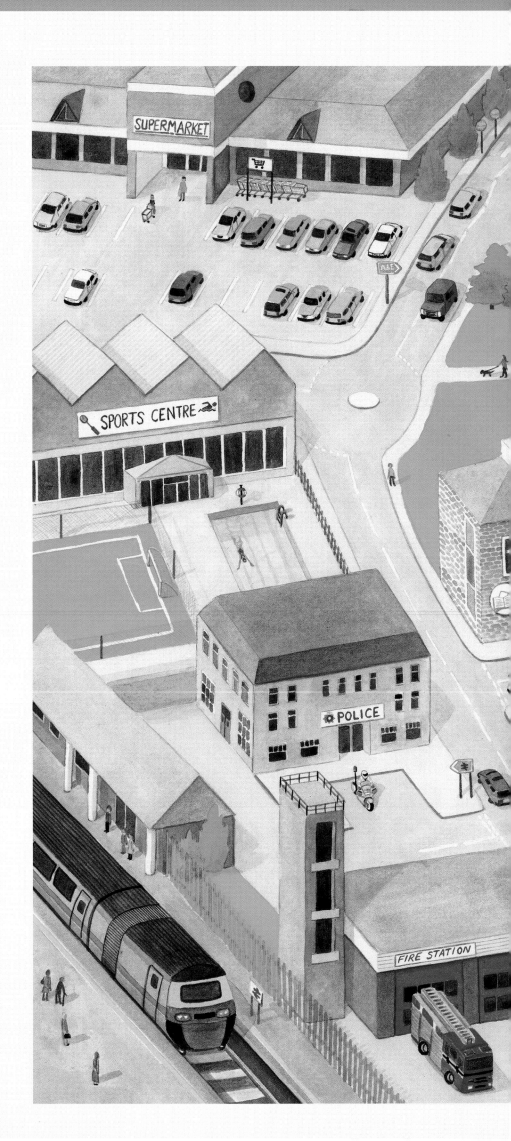

Oraș

spital
spit-al
hospital

parc
park
park

cinema
chinema
cinema

garaj
garazh
garage

stație de autobuz
statsyeh deh ah-oo-tobooz
bus station

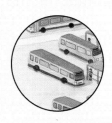

magazine
magazineh
shops/stores

școală
shkwa-luh
school

restaurant
restah-oo-rant
restaurant

florărie
flo-ruh-ryeh
flower shop

vânzător de ziare
vun-zuh-tor deh zee-areh
newsagent

librărie
lee-bruh-ryeh
book shop

măcelărie
muh-cheluh-ryeh
butcher

poștă
posh-tuh
post office

pescărie
pes-kuh-ryeh
fishmonger

Strada principală

aprozar
ah-pro-zahr

greengrocer

farmacie
farm-ah-chyeh

chemist

brutărie
broo-tuh-ryeh

bakery

bancă
bank-uh

bank

magazin de jucării
magazin deh joo-kuh-ree

toyshop

cafenea
cafe-nya

coffee shop

coafor
kwa-for

hairdressers

Road Safety

stradă

stra-duh

road

semafor

sema-for

traffic light

omulețul roșu

o-moo-lets-ool roshoo

red man

omulețul verde

o-moo-lets-ool ver-deh

green man

lumini

loo-meen

lights

reflector

reflec-tor

reflector

cască de ciclist

caskuh deh chy-clist

cycle helmet

trecere de pietoni

tre-chereh deh pee-eh-ton

pedestrian crossing

Siguranța rutieră

mergi
merge
go

oprește
o-pre-shteh
stop

uită-te
ooy-tuh-teh
look

ascultă
ass-cool-tuh
listen

trecere pentru copii
tre-cheh-re
pent-roo copee
children crossing

persoană care se ocupă de trecerea pietonilor în zona școlii
per-swanuh kar seh o-coo-puh deh
tre-chair-ya pee-eh-tony-lor un zonah shko-lee
school crossing patrol officer

centură de siguranță
chent-ooruh deh
see-goorantsuh
seat belt

trotuar
trot-wahr
pavement

Transport

avion
ah-vee-on
aeroplane

camion
kamyon
lorry/truck

mașină
masheenuh
car

autocar
owto-car
coach

barcă
bar-kuh
boat

bicicletă
bee-chy-kletuh
bicycle

tren
trehn
train

Transport

motocicletă
motto-chy-kletuh
motorbike

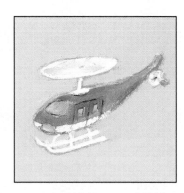

helicopter
heli-koptehr
helicopter

autobuz
owto-booz
bus

tramvai
tram-vy
tram

rulotă
roo-lotuh
caravan

vapor
vah-por
ship

ricșă
rick-shuh
rickshaw

Farm Animals

pasăre
passureh
bird

cal
kal
horse

rață
ra-tsuh
duck

pisică
pee-see-cuh
cat

capră
kapruh
goat

iepure
yeh-poo-re
rabbit

vulpe
vool-peh
fox

Animale domestice

vacă
vakuh
cow

câine
cuh-ineh
dog

oaie
wa-yeh
sheep

șoarice
shwa-ree-cheh
mouse

closcă
closh-kuh
hen

măgar
muh-gar
donkey

gâscă
guhs-kuh
goose

Wild Animals

maimuță
my-moo-tsuh
monkey

elefant
eleh-fant
elephant

șarpe
shar-peh
snake

zebră
zeh-bruh
zebra

leu
leh-oo
lion

hipopotam
hee-popo-tam
hippopotamus

delfin
del-phin
dolphin

balenă
balehnuh
whale

Animale sălbatice

panda
panda
panda bear

girafă
giraffuh
giraffe

cămilă
kuh-mee-luh
camel

tigru
tee-groo
tiger

urs
oors
bear

pinguin
pin-goo-in
penguin

crocodil
croco-dill
crocodile

rechin
reh-kin
shark

Seaside

mare
mareh
sea

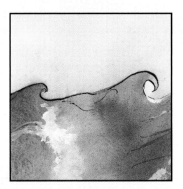

valuri
val-oor
waves

plajă
pla-zhuh
beach

salvamar
sal-văh-mar
lifeguard

loțiune de plajă
lotsy-ooneh deh plazhuh
sun lotion

scoici
skoych
shells

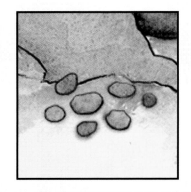

pietriș
pyeh-trish
pebbles

alge de mare
alge deh mareh
seaweed

La mare

baltă între pietre
baltuh untreh pyeh-tre
rock pool

crab
crab
crab

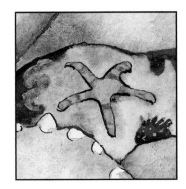

stea de mare
st-ya deh mareh
starfish

șezlong
chez-long
deckchair

nisip
nee-sip
sand

castel de nisip
cast-ell deh nee-sip
sandcastle

găleată
guh-lyatuh
bucket

lopată
lop-atuh
spade

Playground

leagăn
lya-guhn
swing

carusel
carousel
roundabout

balansoar
balanswar
seesaw

groapă cu nisip
grwa-puh koo nee-sip
sandpit

tunel
toonel
tunnel

înăuntru
unuh-oont-roo
in

afară
a-faruh
out

săritură
suh-rit-ooruh
skip

schelet de cățărat
skelet deh cuh-tsuh-rat

climbing frame

sus
soos

up

topogan
topo-gun

slide

jos
zhos

down

peste
pest-eh

over

dedesupt
deh-deh-soopt

under

în față
un fatsuh

in front

în spate
un spat-eh

behind

Classroom

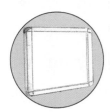

tablă albă
ta-bluh albuh
white board

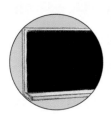

tablă neagră
ta-bluh nya-gruh
chalk board

bancă
bankuh
desk

scaun
skawn
chair

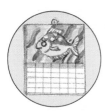

calendar
calendahr
calendar

casetofon
casetto-phon
tape recorder

casetă
casettuh
cassette tape

computer
com-pew-ter
calculator

În clasă

profesor
pro-feh-sore
teacher

cărți
curts
books

hârtie
hur-tyeh
paper

vopsea
vop-sya
paint

pensulă
pen-sooluh
paintbrush

foarfece
fwar- feh-ch
scissors

lipici
leep-itch
glue

bandă lipicioasă
banduh leep-itch-wasuh
sticky tape

School Bag

caiet
ka-yet
writing book

manual de matematică
ma-noo-ahl deh mateh-matikuh
maths book

mapă
map-uh
folder

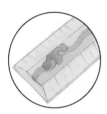

liniar
lee-nee-ar
ruler

raportor
rah-port-or
protractor

creion
crayon
pencil

ascuțitoare
ass-kootsy-twa-re
pencil sharpener

Ghiozdan

manual de lectură
mah-noo-ahl deh leck-tooruh
reading book

pastel
past-ell
crayon

sfoară
sf-waruh
string

bani
bun
money

compas
kompass
compass

gumă
goomuh
rubber/eraser

carioca
carrry-oka
felt tip pen

Computers

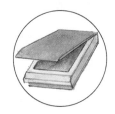

scaner
scanner
scanner

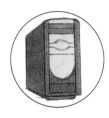

calculator
kal-cool-ate-war
computer

monitor
moni-tor
monitor

tastatură
tass-tah-too-ruh
keyboard

mouse
mouse
mouse

suport pentru mouse
sou-port pent-roo mouse
mouse mat

Calculatoare

imprimantă
imp-ree-man-tuh
printer

ecran
ek-run
screen

internet
internet
internet

email
email
email

CD
CD
cd disc

dischetă
disketuh
floppy disc

Dressing Up

astronaut
astro-nowt
astronaut

poliţist
poly-tsi-st
police person

veterinar
veh-ter-in -ar
vet

pompier
pom-pee-er
firefighter

pictor
pick-tor
artist

vânzător
vun-zuh-tor
shop keeper

jocheu
zho-keh-oo
jockey

cowboy
cowboy
cowboy

bucătar
bookuh-tar
chef

Costumare

soră medicală
soruh medi-kaluh
nurse

mecanic auto
mechanic owto
car mechanic

conducător de tren
con-doo-kuh-tor deh trehn
train driver

balerină
balet-ree-nuh
ballet dancer

vedetă pop
veh-deh-tuh pop
pop star

claun
clown
clown

pirat
pee-rat
pirate

vrăjitor
vruh-zhy-tor
wizard

doctor
doctor
doctor

Toys and Games

balon
bal-on
balloon

mărgele
muhr-ge-leh
beads

joc
zhok
board game

păpușă
puh-poo-shuh
doll

casă de păpuși
casuh deh puh-poosh
doll's house

zmeu
zmeh-oo
kite

puzzle
puzzle
puzzle

coardă
cwar-duh
skipping rope

titirez
tee-tee-rez
spinning top

cuburi
koo-boo-ry
building blocks

șah
shah
chess

zar
zar
dice

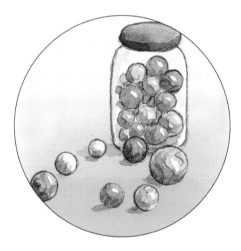

bile de sticlă
bill-eh deh stikluh
marbles

cărți de joc
kuhrts deh zhok
playing cards

marionetă
marionette-uh
puppet

ursuleț
oor-sool-ets
teddy bear

set de tren
set deh trehn
train set

mașinuță
machine-ootsuh
toy car

Sport

baschetbol
basketball
basketball

minge
meen-ge
ball

crichet
cricket
cricket

badminton
badminton
badminton

înot
unot
swimming

patine cu rotile
patineh coo rot-eel-eh
roller skates

rachetă
racquetuh
racquet

patine
pat-ee-neh
ice skates

tenis
tennis
tennis

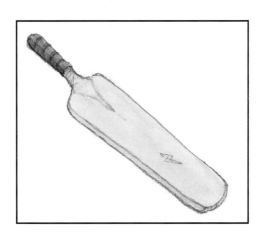

baston
bass-ton
bat

netbol
netball
netball

fotbal
faut-bal
football

ciclism
chy-klism
cycling

rugby
roogby
rugby

skate-board
skateboard
skateboard

hochei
hockay
hockey

Music

tobă
tobuh
drum

tabla
tabla
tabla

clarinet
clarinet
clarinet

flaut
flowt
flute

harpă
harpuh
harp

claviatură
cla-vee-ate-ooruh
keyboard

ghitară
guitar-uh
guitar

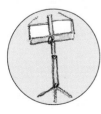

portativ
portative
music stand

Muzică

trianglu muzical
tri-angloo moozik-ahl
musical triangle

trompetă
trom-pet-uh
trumpet

maracas
maracas
maracas

gan gan
gan-gan
gan gan

pian
pee-ann
piano

fluier
floo-yehr
recorder

vioară
vee-waruh
violin

xilofon
ksee-lo-phone
xylophone

Space

soare
swa-reh
sun

Mercur
mer-koor
Mercury

Venus
venus
Venus

Pământ
pumunt
Earth

luna
loona
moon

navă spaţială
na-vuh spa-tsy-aluh
spaceship

stea căzătoare
stya kuh-zuh-twa-reh
shooting star

rachetă
racquetuh
rocket

Marte
mar-teh
Mars

Jupiter
zhoopiter
Jupiter

Saturn
satoorn
Saturn

Uranus
oora-noos
Uranus

cometă
cometuh
comet

stele
steh-leh
stars

Neptun
neptoon
Neptune

Pluto
plooto
Pluto

51

Weather

însorat
un-sore-at
sunny

curcubeu
koor-koo-beh-oo
rainbow

ploios
ploy-oss
rainy

tunet
toon-eht
thunder

fulger
fool-ger
lightning

furtunos
foor-toon-oss
stormy

vântos
vun-toss
windy

cețos
che-tsos
foggy

ninsoare
neen-swa-reh
snowy

înorat
unorat
cloudy

grindină
green-dinuh
hail

ghețuș
gye-tsoosh
icy

Months of the Year

Lunile anului

ianuarie
yan-waryeh
January

februarie
febr-waryeh
February

martie
martyeh
March

aprilie
apreelyeh
April

mai
my
May

iunie
yoonyeh
June

iulie
yoolyeh
July

august
owgoost
August

septembrie
septembryeh
September

octombrie
oktombryeh
October

noiembrie
noy-embryeh
November

decembrie
dechembryeh
December

Seasons

Anotmpuri

primăvară	vară	toamnă	iarnă	muson
preemuh-varuh	varuh	twamnuh	yarnuh	mooson
Spring	**Summer**	**Autumn/Fall**	**Winter**	**Monsoon**

Days of the Week

Zilele săptămânii

luni
loon
Monday

marți
marts
Tuesday

miercuri
myerkoor
Wednesday

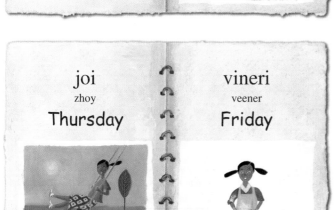

joi
zhoy
Thursday

vineri
veener
Friday

sâmbătă
sumbutuh
Saturday

duminică
doo-meen-eekuh
Sunday

Telling the Time

Spunând ora

ceas
chass
clock

zi
zee
day

noapte
nwapteh
night

dimineață
dee-mee-nyatsuh
morning

seară
syaruh
evening

ceas de mână
chass deh munuh
watch

și un sfert
shee oon sfert
quarter past

și jumătate
shee zhoomutateh
half past

fără un sfert
furuh oon sfert
quarter to

Colours

Culori

roșu
ro-shoo
red

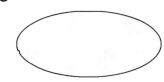

portocaliu
porto-kal-yoo
orange

galben
gall-ben
yellow

verde
ver-deh
green

negru
negroo
black

alb
alb
white

gri
gree
grey

albastru
alb-ass-trou
blue

mov
mauve
purple

roz
rose
pink

maro
mar-oh
brown

Shapes

Forme

cerc
cherk
circle

stea
stya
star

triunghi
try-oongy
triangle

oval
ovahl
oval

con
cone
cone

dreptunghi
drehpt-oongy
rectangle

pătrat
puht-rat
square

Numbers 1-20

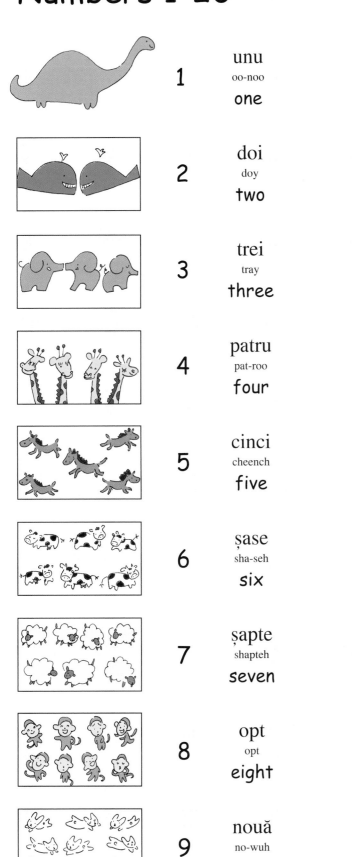

1 — **unu**
oo-noo
one

2 — **doi**
doy
two

3 — **trei**
tray
three

4 — **patru**
pat-roo
four

5 — **cinci**
cheench
five

6 — **șase**
sha-seh
six

7 — **șapte**
shapteh
seven

8 — **opt**
opt
eight

9 — **nouă**
no-wuh
nine

10 — **zece**
zecheh
ten

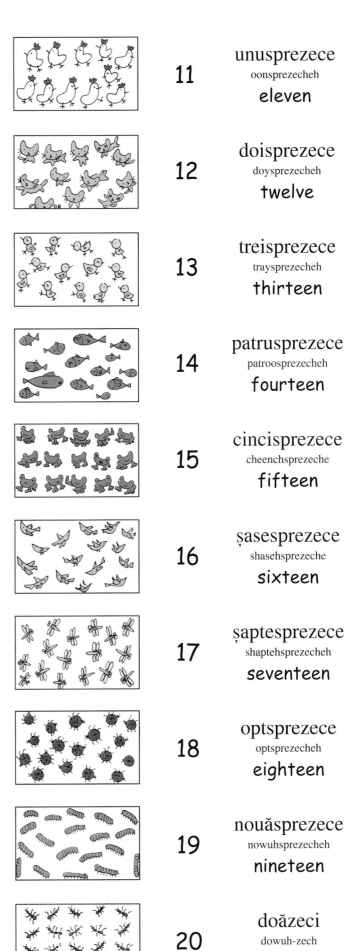

11 — **unusprezece**
oonsprezecheh
eleven

12 — **doisprezece**
doysprezecheh
twelve

13 — **treisprezece**
traysprezecheh
thirteen

14 — **patrusprezece**
patroosprezecheh
fourteen

15 — **cincisprezece**
cheenchsprezeche
fifteen

16 — **șasesprezece**
shasehsprezeche
sixteen

17 — **șaptesprezece**
shaptehsprezecheh
seventeen

18 — **optsprezece**
optsprezecheh
eighteen

19 — **nouăsprezece**
nowuhsprezecheh
nineteen

20 — **doăzeci**
dowuh-zech
twenty

Opposites

repede
reh-pedeh
fast

încet
unchet
slow

deschis
dehskees
open

închis
unkees
closed

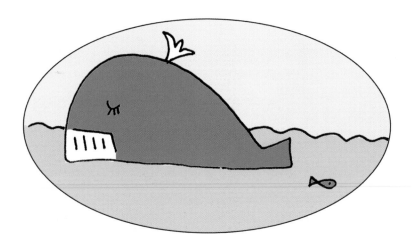

mare
mareh
large

mic
mick
small

ud
wood
wet

uscat
oos-cat
dry

cald
kald
hot

frig
freeg
cold

dulce
doolch
sweet

acru
a-croo
sour

Cuvinte opuse

aproape
ahprwapeh
near

departe
deh-parteh
far

stânga
stunga
left

dreapta
dryaptah
right

față
fatsuh
front

spate
spateh
back

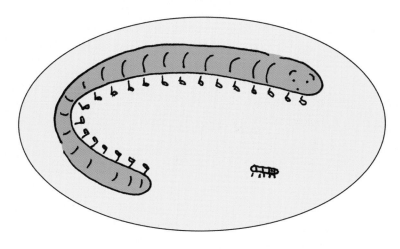

lung
loong
long

scurt
skoort
short

greu
greh-oo
heavy

ușor
oo-shor
light

gol
goal
empty

plin
pleen
full

Index

Search for a word by picture or by the English word

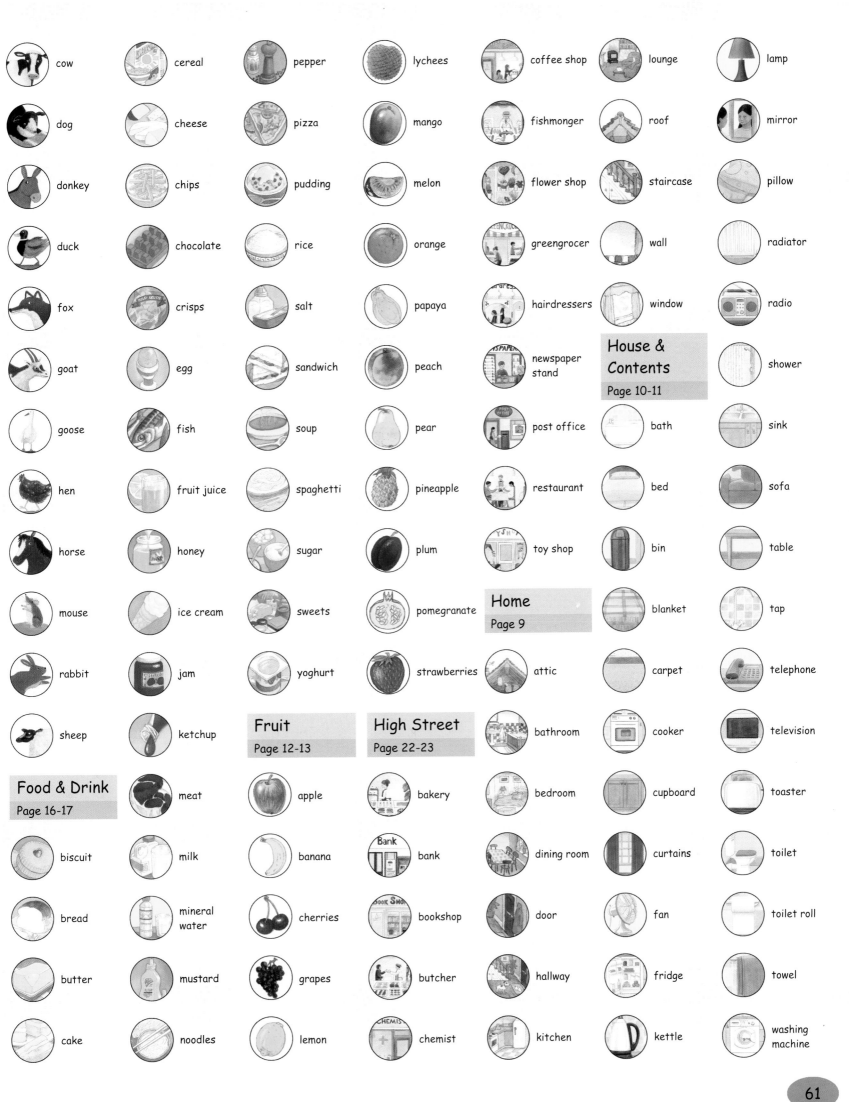

cow

dog

donkey

duck

fox

goat

goose

hen

horse

mouse

rabbit

sheep

Food & Drink
Page 16-17

biscuit

bread

butter

cake

cereal

cheese

chips

chocolate

crisps

egg

fish

fruit juice

honey

ice cream

jam

ketchup

meat

milk

mineral water

mustard

noodles

pepper

pizza

pudding

rice

salt

sandwich

soup

spaghetti

sugar

sweets

yoghurt

Fruit
Page 12-13

apple

banana

cherries

grapes

lemon

lychees

mango

melon

orange

papaya

peach

pear

pineapple

plum

pomegranate

strawberries

High Street
Page 22-23

bakery

bank

bookshop

butcher

chemist

coffee shop

fishmonger

flower shop

greengrocer

hairdressers

newspaper stand

post office

restaurant

toy shop

Home
Page 9

attic

bathroom

bedroom

dining room

door

hallway

kitchen

lounge

roof

staircase

wall

window

House & Contents
Page 10-11

bath

bed

bin

blanket

carpet

cooker

cupboard

curtains

door

fan

fridge

kettle

lamp

mirror

pillow

radiator

radio

shower

sink

sofa

table

tap

telephone

television

toaster

toilet

toilet roll

towel

washing machine

61

Meal Time
Page 18-19

bowl
chopsticks
cup
flask
fork
frying pan
glass
knife
lunchbox
mug
plate
saucepan
spoon
wok

Months of the Year
Page 54

January
February
March
April
May
June
July
August
September
October
November
December

Music
Page 48-49

clarinet
drum
flute
gan gan
guitar
harp
keyboard
maracas
musical triangle
music stand
piano
recorder
tabla
trumpet
violin
xylophone

Myself
Page 4-5

angry
ankle
arm
back
ears
elbow
excited
eyes
face
feet
fingers
hair
hand
happy
head
hungry
jealous
knee
leg
mouth
neck
nose
sad
scared
shoulders
shy
sick
stomach
teeth
thumb
tired
toes
waist
wrist

Numbers 1-20
Page 57

one
two
three
four
five
six
seven
eight
nine
ten
eleven
twelve
thirteen
fourteen
fifteen
sixteen
seventeen
eighteen
nineteen
twenty

Opposites
Page 58-59

back
closed
cold
dry
empty
far
fast
front
full
heavy
hot
large
left
light
long
near

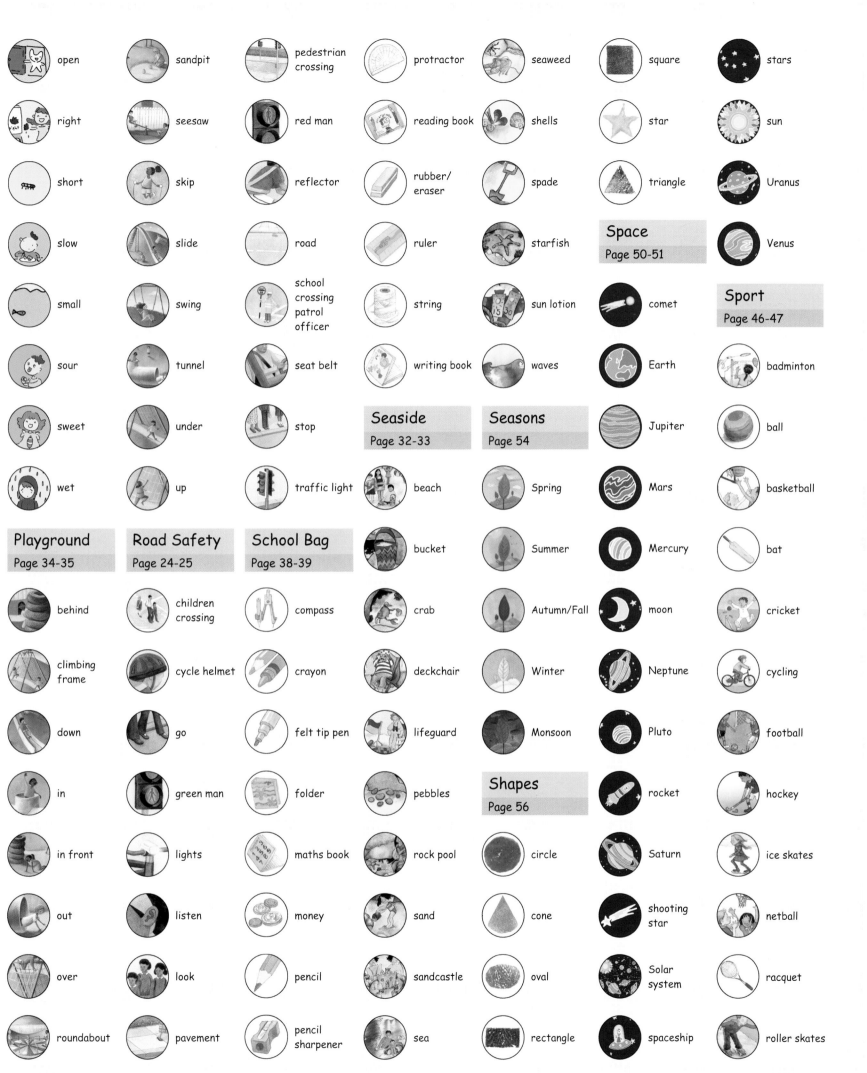

open	sandpit	pedestrian crossing	protractor	seaweed	square	stars
right	seesaw	red man	reading book	shells	star	sun
short	skip	reflector	rubber/eraser	spade	triangle	Uranus
slow	slide	road	ruler	starfish	**Space** Page 50-51	Venus
small	swing	school crossing patrol officer	string	sun lotion	comet	**Sport** Page 46-47
sour	tunnel	seat belt	writing book	waves	Earth	badminton
sweet	under	stop	**Seaside** Page 32-33	**Seasons** Page 54	Jupiter	ball
wet	up	traffic light	beach	Spring	Mars	basketball

Playground Page 34-35 | **Road Safety** Page 24-25 | **School Bag** Page 38-39

behind	children crossing	compass	crab	Summer	Mercury	bat
climbing frame	cycle helmet	crayon	deckchair	Autumn/Fall	moon	cricket
down	go	felt tip pen	lifeguard	Winter	Neptune	cycling
in	green man	folder	pebbles	Monsoon	Pluto	football
in front	lights	maths book	**Shapes** Page 56	rocket	hockey
out	listen	money	rock pool	circle	Saturn	ice skates
over	look	pencil	sand	cone	shooting star	netball
roundabout	pavement	pencil sharpener	sandcastle	oval	Solar system	racquet
			sea	rectangle	spaceship	roller skates

rugby

 cinema

 chess

 boat

 cucumber

 foggy

 crocodile

 skateboard

 fire station

 dice

 bus

 garlic

 hail

 dolphin

 swimming

 garage

 doll

 car

 lettuce

 icy

 elephant

 tennis

 hospital

 doll's house

 caravan

 mushroom

 lightning

 giraffe

Telling the Time
Page 55

 library

 kite

 coach

 onion

 rainbow

 hippopotamus

 clock

 park

 marbles

 helicopter

 peas

 rainy

 lion

 day

 police station

 playing cards

 lorry/truck

 pepper/capsicum

 snowy

 monkey

 evening

 school

 puppet

 motorbike

 potato

 stormy

 panda bear

 half past

 shops/stores

 puzzle

 rickshaw

 pumpkin/squash

 sunny

 penguin

 morning

 sports centre

 skipping rope

 ship

 radish

 thunder

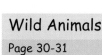 shark

 night

 supermarket

 spinning top

 train

 sweetcorn

 windy

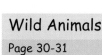 snake

 quarter past

 train station

 teddy bear

 tram

 tomato

Wild Animals
Page 30-31

 tiger

 quarter to

Toys and Games
Page 44-45

 train set

Vegetables
Page 14-15

Weather
Page 52-53

 bear

 whale

 watch

 balloon

 toy car

 beans

 cloudy

 camel

 zebra

Town
Page 20-21

 beads

Transport
Page 26-27

 broccoli

 bus station

 board game

 aeroplane

 carrot

 car park

 building blocks

 bicycle

 cauliflower